GROSS JOBS in SCIENCE

by Nikki Bruno

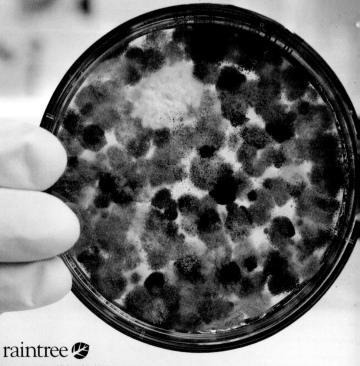

raintree
a Capstone company — publishers for children

Raintree is an imprint of Capstone Global Library Limited, a company incorporated in England and Wales having its registered office at 264 Banbury Road, Oxford, OX2 7DY – Registered company number: 6695582

www.raintree.co.uk
myorders@raintree.co.uk

Edited by Hank Musolf
Designed by Bobbie Nuytten
Original illustrations © Capstone Global Library Limited 2019
Picture research by Heather Mauldin
Production by Katy LaVigne
Originated by Capstone Global Library Ltd
Printed and bound in India

ISBN 978 1 4747 7508 3 (hardbacks)   ISBN 978 1 4747 7017 0 (paperback)
22 21 20 19 18   23 22 21 20 19
10 9 8 7 6 5 4 3 2 1   10 9 8 7 6 5 4 3 2 1

British Library Cataloguing in Publication Data
A full catalogue record for this book is available from the British Library.

Acknowledgements
We would like to thank the following for permission to reproduce photographs:
Alamy: Planetpix, 20 (inset); Getty Images: CHRIS KLEPONIS/AFP, 26 (inset), David Butow/Corbis, 16-17, Matt Cardy/Stringer, 26-27, Wes Pope/Chicago Tribune, 22-23; iStockphoto: AndreasReh, cover, 1, GregorBister, 6-7, Ivan Chudakov, 28-29, KanPhotos, 25, txking, 9; Reuters Pictures: Toshiyuki Aizawa, 19; Shutterstock: Couperfield, 12-13, Fat Jackey, 6 (inset), Laurens Hoddenbagh, 14-15, Lewis Tse Pui Lung, 18, Nyrok555, 20-21, PONG HANDSOME, 10-11, PRESSLAB, 4-5, SGr, 24. Design Elements: Shutterstock: Alhovik, kasha_malasha, Katsiaryna Chumakova, Yellow Stocking.

CONTENTS

WORKING IN SCIENCE

Scientists learn important things from their work. But they're not always wearing white coats in clean labs. Scientists get close to creepy insects. They grow stinky flowers. They even collect poo and make people vomit!

POO SHAKER

Biologists study living creatures. They collect poo to learn about animals' diets and diseases. Poo shakers get the poo ready for research. They shake it in a liquid. Then they can see all the pieces under a **microscope**.

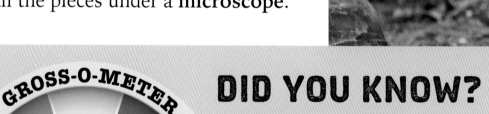

GROSS-O-METER

DID YOU KNOW?

The amount of certain chemicals in an animal's poo can show its level of stress.

microscope tool that makes very small things look large enough to be seen

ARMPIT SNIFFER

Deodorant makes people smell better. But first, someone has to make sure it works. This is a scent researcher's job. They smell people's armpits to test new deodorants. If the product fails, they're in for a nose full of stink!

GROSS-O-METER

DID YOU KNOW?

Scent researchers also study bad breath and mouthwash. Causes of bad breath include **bacteria**, dry mouth and certain foods or medicines.

bacteria very small living things that exist all around you and inside you; some bacteria cause disease

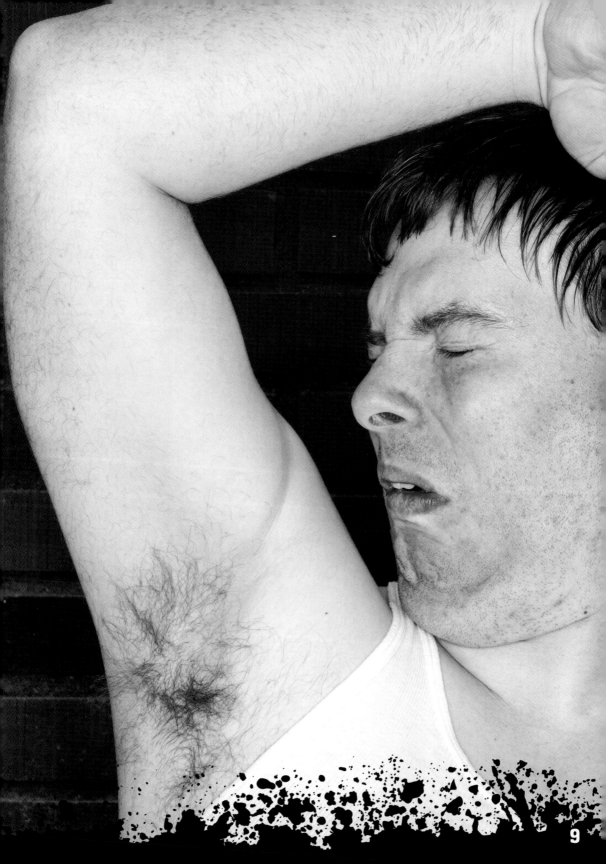

NAUSEA RESEARCHER

Nausea is tummy trouble. People feel nausea before they vomit. This feeling is common for people on spacecraft, aeroplanes and boats. Nausea researchers test new vehicles. Their passengers vomit all the time!

GROSS-O-METER

DID YOU KNOW?

Astronauts often feel nausea when they arrive in space. They vomit in special "sick bags".

nausea feeling of sickness in the stomach

INSECT DETECTIVE

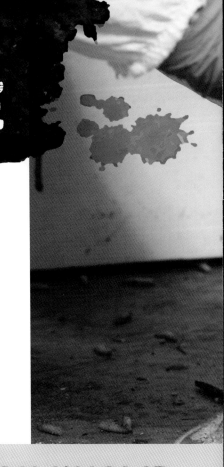

Forensic entomologists are insect detectives. They study bugs on dead bodies. These scientists look at the number and size of **maggots** on a dead body. This tells them how long a person has been dead.

GROSS-O-METER

DID YOU KNOW?

Blowflies are usually the first bugs to arrive on a dead body. They lay eggs in dark, moist places such as the eyes or nose.

maggot larva of certain flies

FUNGUS EXPERT

Mycologists are **fungus** experts. They brave many gross sights and smells in the name of science. Mycologists study fuzzy mould growing on old bread, oozing mushrooms and crusty foot infections.

GROSS-O-METER

DID YOU KNOW?

The largest living thing on Earth is a fungus. It covers 2,385 acres of forest land in Oregon, USA.

fungus organism that has no leaves, flowers or roots; mushrooms and moulds are fungi

MICROBE CHASER

Mono Lake in California, USA, is one of Earth's grossest places. The air and mud smell like rotten eggs, farts and dead fish. Who would go here? **Microbe** chasers! These scientists study tiny creatures that live in the mud.

POISON EATERS

GROSS-O-METER

The Mono Lake microbes eat **arsenic**. This material is poisonous. Microbe chasers are on an important mission. Understanding why these microbes can safely eat poison can help scientists better understand life on Earth.

microbe living thing that is too small to be seen without a microscope

arsenic type of poison

INSECT BREEDER

Did you know insects are worth money? People feed insects to pet snakes and farm animals. Even humans eat insects, either whole or ground into flour. Some scientists **breed** insects. They are surrounded by crawling, flying, wriggling creatures.

GROSS-O-METER

DID YOU KNOW?

On the Indonesian island of Bali, people boil dragonflies in coconut milk, garlic and ginger.

breed mate and raise a certain type of animal

VOLCANO HUNTER

Even exciting jobs can be gross. Volcano scientists lead a life of adventure. But volcanoes aren't just dangerous. They can also be super stinky. Volcanoes shoot out a poisonous gas containing **sulphur**. It smells like rotten eggs.

GROSS-O-METER

DID YOU KNOW?

The sulphur in volcano gas isn't just smelly. It causes coughing and burning in the throat.

sulphur yellow chemical sometimes used to treat skin diseases

PARASITE SCIENTIST

Parasites can be worms, insects, fish or even plants. They **invade** other living things and feed off them. Parasite scientists study eggs buried in poo. They even see worms crawl out of people's skin.

GROSS-O-METER

DID YOU KNOW?

The Guinea worm enters the human body in drinking water. This parasite grows to about 1 metre (3 feet) long inside the **intestine**.

parasite animal or plant that lives on another animal or plant

invade disturb or spread into in a harmful way

intestine long tube that carries and digests food and stores waste products

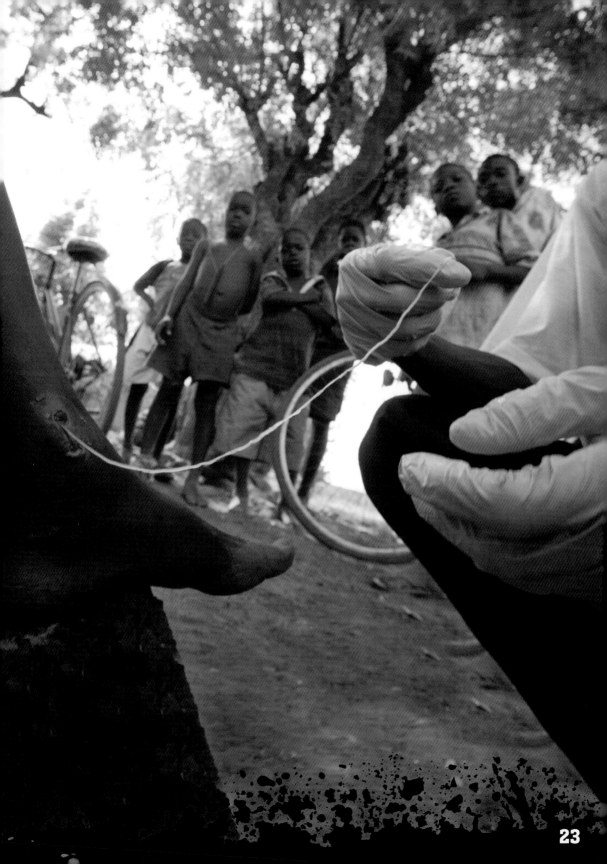

MANURE INSPECTOR

If **manure** contains disease-causing germs, plants that grow in it will have the germs too. Manure inspectors walk into piles of farm-animal poo. They collect samples. They test the samples for bacteria and other causes of disease.

GROSS-O-METER

DID YOU KNOW?

There are nearly 5 million pigs in the UK. They produce almost 4 million tonnes of manure every year.

manure animal droppings that people mix with soil

CORPSE FLOWER GROWER

Most flowers smell lovely. But the corpse flower smells like rotting meat! This flower takes years to bloom. It stays open for only a day or two. Scientists research it quickly. Imagine 24 hours of constant stink!

MONSTER PLANT!

Corpse flowers are enormous. They can reach 2 to 3.6 metres (7 to 12 feet) tall. The plant can weigh more than 113 kilograms (250 pounds).

GROSS-O-METER

THANK YOU SCIENTISTS!

Some scientists surround themselves with gross sights and smells. In the process, they make big discoveries. Thanks to scientists who aren't afraid to get gross, our world is a better place.

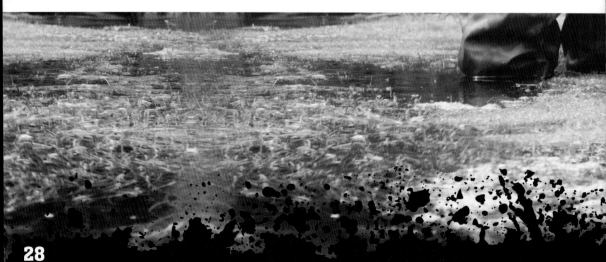

GLOSSARY

arsenic type of poison

bacteria very small living things that exist all around you and inside you; some bacteria cause disease

breed mate and raise a certain type of animal

fungus organism that has no leaves, flowers or roots; mushrooms and moulds are fungi

intestine long tube that carries and digests food and stores waste products

invade disturb or spread into in a harmful way

maggot larva of certain flies

manure animal droppings that people mix with soil

microbe living thing that is too small to see without a microscope

microscope tool that makes very small things look large enough to be seen

nausea feeling of sickness in the stomach

parasite animal or plant that lives on another animal or plant

sulphur yellow chemical sometimes used to treat skin diseases

FIND OUT MORE

BOOKS

Microscopic Monsters (Horrible Science), Nick Arnold (Scholastic, 2018)

Poo and Puke Eaters of the Animal World (Disgusting Creature Diets), Jody Sullivan Rake (Raintree, 2015)

Volcanologist (The Coolest Jobs on the Planet), Hugh Tuffen and Melanie Waldron (Raintree, 2015)

WEBSITES

www.bbc.com/bitesize/articles/zg2g7p3
Learn more about what happens to food in your stomach.

www.dkfindout.com/uk/gallery/science/other-microscope-views
Take a look at some microscope views, including a view of human sweat!

INDEX